PHILANTHROPIC STUDIES

PHILANTH
IN TH
WORLD
TRADITI

PHILANTHROPY
IN THE
WORLD'S
TRADITIONS

Edited by

Warren F. Ilchman,
Stanley N. Katz,
and
Edward L. Queen II

INDIANA UNIVERSITY PRESS   BLOOMINGTON AND INDIANAPOLIS

6-29-99

This book is a publication of

Indiana University Press
601 North Morton Street
Bloomington, Indiana 47404-3797 USA

www.indiana.edu/~iupress

Telephone orders   800-842-6796
Fax orders   812-855-7931
Orders by e-mail   iuporder@indiana.edu

The paper used in this publication meets the minimum
requirements of American National Standard for
Information Sciences—Permanence of Paper for Printed
Library Materials, ANSI Z39.48–1984.

Manufactured in the United States of America.

Library of Congress Cataloging-in-Publication Data

Philanthropy in the world's traditions / edited by Warren F. Ilchman,
Stanley N. Katz, and Edward L. Queen, II.
p.   cm.
Includes bibliographical references and index.
ISBN 0-253-33392-X (cl : alk. paper)
1. Charities—Cross-cultural studies.   2. Charities—History—
Cross-cultural studies.   3. Social service—Cross-cultural studies.
4. Social service—History—Cross-cultural studies.   5. Social
service—Religious aspects.   I. Ilchman, Warren Frederick.
II. Katz, Stanley Nider.   III. Queen, Edward L.
HV16.P46   1998
361.7'632'09—dc21   97-51241

1 2 3 4 5   03 02 01 00 99 98